DAVID STOREY

CROMWELL

D0931049

JONATHAN CAPE
THIRTY BEDFORD SQUARE LONDON

FIRST PUBLISHED 1973
© 1973 BY DAVID STOREY

JONATHAN CAPE LTD
30 BEDFORD SQUARE, LONDON WC1

ISBN Hardback 0 224 00871 4
Paperback 0 224 00873 0

PRINTED IN GREAT BRITAIN
BY EBENEZER BAYLIS & SON LTD
THE TRINITY PRESS, WORCESTER, AND LONDON
ON PAPER MADE BY JOHN DICKINSON & CO. LTD
BOUND BY G. & J. KITCAT LTD, LONDON

CHARACTERS

LOGAN

O'HALLORAN

MORGAN

PROCTOR

CHAMBERLAIN

MOORE

MATHEW

MARGARET

JOAN

KENNEDY

BROOME

CLEET

WALLACE

DRAKE

BOATMAN

FIRST SOLDIER

SECOND SOLDIER

FIRST TRAVELLER

SECOND TRAVELLER

THIRD TRAVELLER

CROWD

ACT ONE

Scene 1

A stage. LOGAN *enters, rubbing his hands: Irish, in his thirties.*

LOGAN. Don't they ever heat this place?
  (*He's followed in by* O'HALLORAN, *also Irish.*)
O'HALLORAN. Not if they can help it ... Anybody up there, is there?
LOGAN (*gazing*). No. No. Not a thing. (*Calls*) Anybody up there, is there?
  (*Pause.*)
O'HALLORAN. No answer.
LOGAN. Nothing.
O'HALLORAN. Not a person.
LOGAN. Jesus, but it's bloody cold.
O'HALLORAN. Here ... here! Go on, then. Have a tap!
  (*Holds up flat of his hand: they start sparring.*)
  (MORGAN *comes in.*)
MORGAN. Always fighting.
LOGAN. What?
O'HALLORAN. What's that?
LOGAN. Fight you, young man, if you don't watch out.
MORGAN. One hand behind my back, or both?
LOGAN. You or me, O'Halloran?
O'HALLORAN. No, no. Age before beauty, Patrick, every time.
MORGAN. Go on, go on. (*Holds chin out.*)
LOGAN. Ah, now, er ... a little to the left ... No, no. The right.
O'HALLORAN. More in the middle.
LOGAN. More in the middle, now ... that's right.

7

(MORGAN *has swivelled his chin from left to right: now holds it up even more invitingly*.)

Right hand, now, or left ... Should get us warm this, Stephen.

O'HALLORAN. Oh, undoubtedly ...

LOGAN. Should I falter ...

O'HALLORAN. Could always carry on.

LOGAN. That's right.

O'HALLORAN. Ready, Morgan, are you?

MORGAN. Ready? I've been ready half an hour.

LOGAN. Upper cut or overarm, O'Halloran?

O'HALLORAN. Oh, overarm! ... Then, again: the uppercut has a great deal to recommend it.

LOGAN. I think you're right ... the short left jab has always been my favourite.

O'HALLORAN. More a defensive blow, I thought.

LOGAN. More a defensive blow: you're right.

O'HALLORAN. Left hook, now, is a different matter.

LOGAN. Left hook, you know: I think you're right.

O'HALLORAN. Or the old one-two.

LOGAN. Ah, God.

O'HALLORAN. Shan't see it's like.

LOGAN. No, no ...

MORGAN. Are you going to take a swipe, or aren't you?

LOGAN. Steady on, now, Morgan.

O'HALLORAN. Doesn't he know we've got all day?

MORGAN. All day for talking ...

O'HALLORAN. Talking?

LOGAN. Talking?

O'HALLORAN. Isn't he aware ...

LOGAN. That there's a great distinction ...

O'HALLORAN. Between talking ...

LOGAN. And discussion.

8

MORGAN. Have you got the guts to have a swipe? (*Holds out chin.*) Go on. Go on ... Left hand or right.

LOGAN. There: there, now. If I hit him as hard as I can ... (*Looks round.*) There's bound to be inquiries.

MORGAN. I think you're suffering from one or two delusions, Logan, if you don't mind my saying so.

LOGAN. Oh, yes.

MORGAN. Not least, that you've got the courage to hit me on the jaw at all.

LOGAN. I've got the courage, right enough.

O'HALLORAN. And the strength.

LOGAN. And the strength ... What I've got a superabundance of as well ...

MORGAN. Oh, yes?

(LOGAN *looks to* O'HALLORAN. *Then:*)

O'HALLORAN. Compassion.

LOGAN. Compassion.

O'HALLORAN. Compassion, there: I think you're right.

MORGAN. I'm not standing here, you know, all morning.

LOGAN. That's what the English lack.

O'HALLORAN. They do.

LOGAN. Amongst many other things.

MORGAN. What's that?

LOGAN. Ah, now: I don't think it'd be safe to mention it.

O'HALLORAN. No, no: I think you're right.

MORGAN. I'm Welsh.

(O'HALLORAN *and* LOGAN *exchange looks. Silent: they sit, lean back; lounge.*)

LOGAN. Oh, it's a great morning. (*Stretching.*)

O'HALLORAN. A great morning, Patrick, surely ... (*Yawns, stretches.*) A great morning, there ... I think you're right.

(*Light fades.*)

Scene 2

Light comes up.

   LOGAN *and* O'HALLORAN *are lying on the ground;* MORGAN
is sitting, straw in mouth.

   PROCTOR *comes in.*

PROCTOR. Anybody here, then?

O'HALLORAN. No, no ... deserted.

PROCTOR. By God: they tell you get here early ... you come
    on time: no one has arrived.

    (PROCTOR *looks around: stretches: crouches down.*)

LOGAN. They say the feller himself is due past any time.

PROCTOR. You seen him, Mr Logan, have you?

LOGAN. No, no. I never have.

    (PROCTOR *looks to* O'HALLORAN.)

O'HALLORAN. No. No. Me neither.

LOGAN. Mr Morgan?

MORGAN. No ... No.

O'HALLORAN. They say he has an arm ...

MORGAN. Yes?

O'HALLORAN. Twice as thick as his leg.

LOGAN. Is that a fact?

O'HALLORAN. And hair ...

LOGAN. Yes?

O'HALLORAN. I better not describe it.

LOGAN. Oh, now ...

O'HALLORAN. As rough as a witch's broom.

LOGAN. To God.

O'HALLORAN. Can sweep a room ...

LOGAN. No. No. You're telling me ...

O'HALLORAN. As easy as a glance.

    (LOGAN *looks to the others, seemingly amazed.*)

PROCTOR. I saw him once.

LOGAN. Is that a fact?

MORGAN. Is he like O'Halloran says?

PROCTOR. I saw him in the wood ... passing between the trees ... a kind of ...

O'HALLORAN. Mist.

PROCTOR. That's right ...

O'HALLORAN. They say, from a distance – because they'll never let you close – he looks rather like, shall we say ...

LOGAN. A moving vapour.

PROCTOR. It's always misty in the woods ...

O'HALLORAN. People passing by ...

LOGAN. Assume something of the same condition.

O'HALLORAN (*about to add something else—then:*) That's right.

    (LOGAN *whistles a tune: cheerful, perky. Then:*)

MORGAN. We could build a fire.

O'HALLORAN. What's that?

MORGAN. Wood ... There's plenty lying about.

O'HALLORAN. But then ...

LOGAN. We mightn't be here for very long.

O'HALLORAN. No sooner has the wood been laid.

LOGAN. Than along he comes ...

O'HALLORAN. 'And you ... And you ... And you,' he says ...

LOGAN. Up on your feet ...

O'HALLORAN. And off.

LOGAN. And all that wood'll go to waste.

O'HALLORAN. And all the effort with it.

PROCTOR. It's certainly cold. (*Rubbing his hands, he starts to pace.*) Whatever he says ... we can't sit here for long. (*Light slowly fades.*)

Scene 3

Light comes up.
  The men are sitting or lying, silent.
  CHAMBERLAIN *comes in, a well-built, sturdy, middle-aged man.*

CHAMBERLAIN. Are these, then, the only ones who came?
MORGAN. We're the only bloody ones who have.
PROCTOR. Do you know where we have to go?
CHAMBERLAIN. I do.
O'HALLORAN. Come on, then, for God's sake ... sitting here ...
CHAMBERLAIN. You should have been there some time ago.
LOGAN. We've been sitting here ...
O'HALLORAN. We have.
LOGAN. For hours.
O'HALLORAN. Just look at me bloody fingers ...
LOGAN. Dropping off.
O'HALLORAN. Not fit to do a job, we're not.
LOGAN. God: feet likewise. Can hardly stand.
PROCTOR. How far do we have to go?
CHAMBERLAIN. Not far.
MORGAN. Walking, is it? Or do we have a ride?
CHAMBERLAIN. Walking. Unless you've something of your own.
MORGAN. No. No.
LOGAN. No, no.
O'HALLORAN. Too bloody poor.
LOGAN. Too bloody poor. That's right.
O'HALLORAN. Not find a cart, nor animal ... nor anything on four legs round here.
MORGAN. I'm surprised ...
LOGAN. Your honour ...

CHAMBERLAIN. Chamberlain.

MORGAN. Mr Chamberlain, sir, I'm surprised you've not got a conveyance of your own.

CHAMBERLAIN. I had. It was shot away ... There's been fighting in the woods all day. I'm surprised you haven't heard.

O'HALLORAN. We have.

CHAMBERLAIN. You did nothing, then, but sit in here.

LOGAN. Can't fight armed men, you know, with sticks.

CHAMBERLAIN. Some people, I'll have you know, have fought with less ... By the time the sun has set it might be you.

LOGAN. To God.

O'HALLORAN. Come on, for God's sake, then: get off.

CHAMBERLAIN. There was no one in the village but women and children as I was passing through.

PROCTOR. They've all run off.

LOGAN. Except for one or two.

PROCTOR. Except for us.

LOGAN. Damn fine fools we were, I'm thinking.

MORGAN. We were.

LOGAN. To think of even coming here at all.

PROCTOR. Somebody has to stay and fight.

MORGAN. Somebody it could have been: not us.

CHAMBERLAIN. What's your name, then?

PROCTOR. Proctor.

CHAMBERLAIN. Do you have a job?

PROCTOR. I had ... After today, I'm not so sure.

(CHAMBERLAIN *looks to* MORGAN.)

MORGAN. A dairy ... That's to say, two weeks ago I had a cow.

LOGAN. Labourer.

O'HALLORAN. Labourer.

LOGAN. The common kind ...

13

O'HALLORAN. The common kind.

LOGAN. Itinerant.

O'HALLORAN. Itinerant! The very word.

LOGAN. The very phrase I had in mind.

(O'HALLORAN *and* LOGAN *laugh*.)

PROCTOR. I had a smithy: no metal things to mend.

CHAMBERLAIN. No weapons, then?

PROCTOR. No, no. Ploughs there were: a harness, scythes; a metal gate or two.

CHAMBERLAIN. I'm surprised you haven't a horse.

PROCTOR. I had: went the same way as Morgan's cow.

O'HALLORAN. They're eating rats, you know, round here ...

LOGAN. Grass, leaves ...

O'HALLORAN. Even, they tell me, a corpse or two ...

LOGAN. Fresh killed.

O'HALLORAN. Fresh killed.

LOGAN. Or not so fresh.

O'HALLORAN. Or not so fresh. I think he's right.

PROCTOR (*to* CHAMBERLAIN). Will we be fed do you think tonight?

(*No answer:* CHAMBERLAIN *is looking off, preparatory to leaving.*)

Will we be fed, do you think, sir, when we reach this place tonight?

CHAMBERLAIN. We might ... I'm hoping so. (*Looks round: sees them watching him — then:*) If we set off now. I think we might.

MORGAN. Are you walking, then, like us?

CHAMBERLAIN. I have no choice.

O'HALLORAN. Did the feller send for us himself?

CHAMBERLAIN. All able-bodied men ... That's right.

LOGAN. Then that lets you and me out, O'Halloran, for a bloody start.

(*They laugh.*)
Not have to carry you or something? On the back.
CHAMBERLAIN. No, no. I'll walk along. Just like yourselves.
O'HALLORAN. To God, now ... but that's a bloody sight ...
LOGAN. One sent by himself ...
O'HALLORAN. Walking on the track.
LOGAN. Two feet.
O'HALLORAN. Two feet.
LOGAN. And two beautiful, fine, long legs to match.
     (LOGAN *and* O'HALLORAN *laugh.*)
CHAMBERLAIN. Are you ready, then? We've waited here too
     long already.
PROCTOR. Aye ... There's nothing now to keep us here.
CHAMBERLAIN. We'll skirt the woods ... you can show the
     way.
     (O'HALLORAN *starts back.*)
Since you know the place so well, that is.
     (*They begin to leave.*
     Light fades.)

Scene 4

Light comes up.
   *The light comes up on a wooden coffin lying on a cart. There's
   the distant roar of cannon.*
   O'HALLORAN *has come in.*

O'HALLORAN. Jesus now: but there's a rare old sight.
LOGAN (*following him in*). Food at last ...
O'HALLORAN. Cooked, do you think ...
LOGAN. Waitin' to be served.
O'HALLORAN. Undoubtedly someone special.

LOGAN. Somebody very grand!

PROCTOR (*coming in*). That's the first we've seen inside a box.

LOGAN. The lid's been fastened down. (*Trying it.*)

O'HALLORAN (*looks round*). Could hardly have done the thing himself.

LOGAN. No, no. I'd say that someone's done it for him ... Pinned down, he is.

O'HALLORAN. Oh, snug and cosy.

LOGAN. A cart to ride upon, at that.

O'HALLORAN (*as* CHAMBERLAIN *enters, tiredly*). Jesus: but that noise is getting close.

LOGAN. Either that ...

O'HALLORAN. Or my bloody stomach ...

LOGAN. Is grumbling here from lack of food.

(CHAMBERLAIN *looks round.*)

CHAMBERLAIN. Was this standing here, then, unattended?

LOGAN. Aye. It was, it was ... quite on its own. No one to trouble ...

O'HALLORAN. ... Or protect it.

MORGAN (*coming in last, weary*). Have you tried the lid?

O'HALLORAN. He has.

PROCTOR. It's nothing of our concern ... We better leave it.

LOGAN. To God, now, man ... And what about the cart?

CHAMBERLAIN. The one goes with the other, I would have thought.

O'HALLORAN. The one goes with us, I would have thought, might sound a little better.

(O'HALLORAN *joins* LOGAN *to try the coffin.*)

There, now, but that's a weight.

LOGAN. More like two or three, I would have thought, inside.

O'HALLORAN. Proctor: aren't you going to give a soul a hand.

PROCTOR. I've seen enough of the dead and dying ... I've

seen enough for all my life: I'm damned if I want to touch one that's decently encased. Cart or no cart. You can shift the thing yourself.

o'halloran. Morgan ... you Welshy bastard, aren't you going to give a lift?

morgan. And who's to push the bleeding thing: that's what I would like to ask.

o'halloran. We'll take it turn and turn about.

morgan. Aye? And who's to ride on first?

logan. The stringy bastard: I'll lift the thing myself. (*Hoists up one end of the coffin.*)

(moore *comes on: an old man.*)

moore. Would you leave that ... Would you leave it, sir?

o'halloran. To God. And who the hell is this?

moore. I'm the brother of the one inside ... and the cart, like the corpse, your honour, is part of mine.

logan. I'll be damned: but the shape you're in you ought to be in there with him.

o'halloran. Have you pushed the thing yourself?

morgan. I have ... with a little help.

logan. Not from up above, I'm thinking.

moore. No, no ... I have a friend.

(mathew *has come on: a sinewy, ragged, frantic creature.*)

o'halloran. In the same condition as yourself.

moore. We haven't eaten for a day ... And the day before was hardly better ... if we've anything to take, then take it ... But not the cart.

logan. Bejasus: it's not the box we're after.

(mathew *has started making signs.*)

moore. He doesn't speak.

morgan. From choice, you mean.

proctor. No, no, you see ...

chamberlain. The man's afflicted.

logan. To God: he'll defend it with his life! (*Laughs at*

MATHEW's *wild gestures*.) Go on! Go on! Go on there, now! (*Makes gestures to provoke him.*)

O'HALLORAN. One old man, a fool: why don't we bury the thing, and take the cart.

LOGAN. Aye. Aye. We'll dispose of the one ...

O'HALLORAN. And take care of the other.

LOGAN (*to* MOORE). For after that ...

O'HALLORAN. There'll be no need ...

LOGAN. For either of you to want it longer.

(MARGARET *has come in: a middle-aged woman.*)

MARGARET. The body cannot be buried here ... Nor anywhere but on consecrated ground.

O'HALLORAN. Jasus: but how many more have we got to come?

LOGAN. Hiding, are you, in the trees? (*Looking off.*)

MARGARET. There's no one else.

MOORE. This is my niece ... my brother's only child.

O'HALLORAN. More beautiful, I would imagine, than the one inside.

(*He and* LOGAN *laugh.*

MORGAN *has collapsed on the ground, resting.*

PROCTOR, *having already set off, waits now, gazing back.*

CHAMBERLAIN, *though taking in the situation, still watches off.*)

MORGAN. It's the cart they're after, not your father, girl.

PROCTOR (*reapproaching*). If he was so precious, why did you leave him here like this?

MARGARET. We thought it was the soldiers ...

MOORE. Coming through the wood.

(MATHEW *gestures off.*)

O'HALLORAN. Aye. Soldiers we are, I hope, in a couple of hours.

MORGAN. Aye. With a soldier's pay, and a soldier's grub.

LOGAN. Which is not a sentiment, madam, that I share myself.

PROCTOR. There's a church we passed, an hour ago, a priest ... why don't you take him there?

MOORE. That's not a Roman church, you see.

O'HALLORAN. Are you one of us?

MARGARET. We are ... (*She looks from one to the other.*) It seems we are.

LOGAN. And look at this.

O'HALLORAN. Not one more left.

MORGAN. Then where's she from?

(JOAN *has come in: a girl, nineteen or twenty.*)

JOAN. I couldn't wait there any longer. If they're one of us then we've nothing to fear.

(MORGAN *has half got up, rising to his knees.*)

O'HALLORAN. How many more have you got back there?

LOGAN. Is this the first of a regular troupe?

MOORE. These people are under my protection.

MARGARET. This is my daughter: there's no one else.

JOAN. The road's safe, then: these men — they'll let us pass?

O'HALLORAN. Aye, now ... aren't we going the same way, too? ... The cart, if I'm not mistaken, is pointing in the same direction.

CHAMBERLAIN. We've not time to wait with these: it's getting late ... The sun's down now to the tops of the trees.

LOGAN. And which way do we go from here ... ?

CHAMBERLAIN. I thought you knew the route.

LOGAN. I do ...

O'HALLORAN. But not the one, you see, we've taken ... (*To* MOORE, *by whom he's come to stand*) You see, we've been so much hedged about ... cutting this way, cutting that ... avoiding the armies moving in the woods ... that by now we're miles from the road we took. (*Looks about him, head raised*.) You couldn't show us the way, old man, yourself.

MOORE. We've been travelling as it is for several days ...

LOGAN. But that's the smell ... It's pouring from the box! (*Moves back*.) Good God ... Infection, man, you see. Look out!

MOORE. My niece can't let her father rest without the last rites being passed above his head.

MARGARET. Our own priest left.

MOORE. He'd been hiding in the woods for days.

MARGARET. The soldiers came.

JOAN. They searched the farm ...

MARGARET. Fortunately, by then, that night, my father died ... (*To* O'HALLORAN) Since then, you see, we've travelled with the cart.

LOGAN. But then, if the man is one of us ...

O'HALLORAN. Aren't we moving generally — hopefully, Ma'am, I might even say — in the same direction?

LOGAN. A young lady like yourself.

O'HALLORAN. Without protection ...

LOGAN. But for an old man, an idiot ... and an ageing wife.

O'HALLORAN (*to* MARGARET). Your husband, I take it, has been captured like ourselves ... enlisted in the war.

MARGARET. He has ...

JOAN. He volunteered.

MARGARET. It was something he believed in.

JOAN. And now he's dead.

O'HALLORAN. Fatherless as well, to boot ... Morgan ... Get up on your feet, there, man ... Logan: take this side ... and you take this.

MORGAN. And what are you going to do, O'Halloran, yourself?

O'HALLORAN. I shall direct the cart, and watch the track ... avoid the bog-holes, and watch the trees around ... Proctor? Are you going to lend a hand?

PROCTOR. Aye. I suppose there's nothing left to lose … (*To* CHAMBERLAIN) If he's lost the way he'll not direct us back.

LOGAN. Are you coming, Mr Chamberlain? Or will you find your own way on from here?

CHAMBERLAIN. Aye … (*He looks about.*) It's too late now to search round for a track … (*He lifts his head at the sound of guns.*) In any case, when we get there, I've a feeling it's going to be too late.

(*The men have lifted the cart: they set it to the track.*)

O'HALLORAN. Would a fair hand like yours do you think be strong enough to help me with the tiller.

JOAN. Yes. I'll help.

MARGARET. I'll help as well.

O'HALLORAN. No, no, now, lady: you've pushed enough. You walk on with the gentlemen behind …

(MATHEW *has already gripped the side of the cart to push.*) (*To* JOAN) I think, between ourselves, with the help we have in hand, we'll manage … Are you ready, fellers, then? … And … heave!

(*They move off.*
Light fades.)

Scene 5

Light comes up.

O'HALLORAN *and* JOAN *sit on the ground: half-light, and flickering light, off, from a fire.*

Behind them, some distance off, MATHEW *moves up and down, gesturing, restless, as if talking to them, or with himself.*

21

O'HALLORAN. What sort of farm did you have?

JOAN. Oh ... crops ...

O'HALLORAN. Cattle?

JOAN. We had a few ...

O'HALLORAN. I'm a great cattle man, of course, myself.

JOAN. Yes?

O'HALLORAN. There's not many a thing I don't know about cows ... As for beef and bulls ... There's many a man I've never set eyes on come asking for advice.

JOAN. When the soldiers came they drove them off.

O'HALLORAN (*watches her. Then:*) You'll go back there when the old man's safe beneath the ground?

JOAN. I might.

O'HALLORAN. What other places are there, then?

JOAN. I've only known the farm. I couldn't tell.

O'HALLORAN. I've travelled far and wide, meself.

(*She doesn't answer.*)

Do I look a travelled man, d'you think?

JOAN. I don't know ... You look like any other.

O'HALLORAN. Lines of experience ... If the light was a little stronger you could trace them out ... There ... (*Takes her hand: puts it to his face.*) ... Eyes and cheek ... And particularly around the mouth.

(MATHEW *has come closer, gesturing, miming speech.*)

God: that smell is strong ... Wouldn't it be better to bury him, do you think?

JOAN. It depends how strong you feel.

O'HALLORAN. I feel strong enough ... I feel strong enough to put him in the ground meself.

JOAN. My mother can't ... Without a blessing ... Even if there's nothing left but bone: without that he'll find no rest. And without that, *she*'ll find none either.

O'HALLORAN. Superstition ... I'd bury the man myself: put damn stones inside the box ... She'd never know ... And

he's too far gone, I think, to bother much himself ...
There's nothing beyond death, you know.

(JOAN *doesn't answer*.)

And what is there, then, that you could put your finger on
right now?

(*She shakes her head*.)

There's the stars up yonder, there's the two of us down
here ... between the three — them, us and it (*Indicating
coffin*) — can you see anything else intruding? ... Not
counting that raving lunatic o' course.

(*Pause*.)

JOAN. When the soldiers came, the day he died, I saw them
first about a mile away ... on horses ... they came over to
the field at the back of the house: it was full of crops:
potatoes mainly ...

O'HALLORAN. I've seen them across that sort of space myself ... Damn great fellers: like trees, they are ... I've often
thought I'd make a damn fine soldier boy meself ... tall,
handsome ... a commanding presence ... if I could only
keep my backside on top of a horse I'd have been one of
the King's men, I'm thinking, long ago ... I've often
wondered ...

(JOAN *looks across at him*.)

How I've eluded conscription by the army-men so long ...
a natural gift like mine ... you'd imagine they'd have put
it to some militaristic use, now, long ago ... Ah, well ...
it needs an eye to spot an eye ... and if the eyes on one
side, you know, are not so good ... then ones like mine go
unattended.

JOAN. I've seen one die.

O'HALLORAN. What? (*He looks behind him*.)

JOAN. The day they came I found one lying in the hedge ...
he'd got a pipe ... It was the smoke I saw at first ... rising
... a thin blue cloud ... it settled round the twigs and leaves

... 'There's a fire over there,' I thought ... when I went across I saw a boot ... It was sticking out ... It had a hole, the size of this ... in the middle of the sole ... and when I looked between the leaves I saw an eye ...

O'HALLORAN. To God. (*He glances up, behind, at the now still and listening* MATHEW.)

JOAN. At first, I thought he'd been asleep ... eyes open, now, the pipe still in his hand ... When I got up close ...

O'HALLORAN. Go on, go on.

JOAN. I saw his throat.

O'HALLORAN. To God ...

JOAN. From ear to ear.

O'HALLORAN. Is that a fact?

JOAN. The ash had fallen from his pipe ... and started smouldering in the grass ...

O'HALLORAN. Just sitting there: to have a rest. Got out his pipe ...
(*Looks behind:* MATHEW *stands gazing over.*)
What happened then?

JOAN. I saw the soldiers ... riding to the field ... When they came up close I ran back to the house: they were looking at the crops.

O'HALLORAN. For food.

JOAN. Or him ... I warned them at the house, and when I came back out, they were riding by the hedge.

O'HALLORAN. Go on. Go on ...

JOAN. I thought we'd be taken then for sure ... a soldier murdered ... almost at the door ... They rode straight past: came right into the yard ... looking at the spot it seemed itself.

O'HALLORAN. Go on, then, girl. What happened next?

JOAN. They asked what crops we had. They looked inside the house, the barn ... an hour later, when they left, we ran down to the hedge ... (*Looks up at* O'HALLORAN.)

The grass was flattened. Nothing else. A smudge of ash where the pipe had been.

O'HALLORAN. Don't tell me he'd got up and walked away himself.

JOAN. I've no idea.

O'HALLORAN (*looks round him once again*). They're mystical fellers ... I'll grant you that.

JOAN. The soldiers came back an hour later ... By then, my grandfather had been fastened in his coffin ... It would have broken his heart to see the things they took ... The cattle ... They dug the fields ... took all the roots ... there was nothing left ... That night we set off for a priest ... and found he'd fled ... We've been walking ever since ... A week: it must be more ... At first we had some food ... and then ... everywhere we went burnt fields, houses, even churches left in ruins ...

(CHAMBERLAIN *passes across the back*.)

CHAMBERLAIN. I'll put the fire down ... As bright as that we'll soon be seen.

JOAN. Who is he? Is he one of you?

O'HALLORAN. He's the recruiting sergeant, so to speak ... The gentleman who wants to enlist us in his troop sent him off to pick us up, and one or two others who, in the circumstances, thought it discreeter to go wandering in the woods ... His horse got shot away: he escaped himself and, so to speak, lost us as well ... And what do you call the lunatic jumper, then? (*Indicating* MATHEW.)

JOAN. That's Mathew ... He's been with my father all his life.

O'HALLORAN. And you yourself?

JOAN. I'm Joan.

O'HALLORAN. That's a hard, reliable name ... Mine's O'Halloran ... Stephen to my friends ... Your mother's name: I thought I heard it as we came along?

JOAN. Margaret.

O'HALLORAN. If that isn't just as fine a name as well.
(CHAMBERLAIN *has come back.*)

CHAMBERLAIN. I think the firing's dying down.

O'HALLORAN. Either that, or we're going deaf from lack of food.

CHAMBERLAIN. When the sun's up we'll find the road. (*To* JOAN) I'm afraid we'll have to leave you then.

O'HALLORAN. Ah, to God, your honour: they can go with us.

CHAMBERLAIN. Only if our ways combine: their way with ours ... I'll leave you, then ... Keep your voices down ... (*Goes.*)

O'HALLORAN. Don't worry ... No need any more, I think, for words ...
(*Light fades.*)

Scene 6

The light comes up on the cart: pushed by MORGAN, PROCTOR *and* MATHEW)

O'HALLORAN *has come on ahead: pauses. He holds up his hand to halt.*

O'HALLORAN. Jesus, now: but there's someone there ...
(LOGAN, *holding a rope fastened to the cart, comes on behind.*)

PROCTOR. I've heard no firing now for hours.

LOGAN. The battle's over: I think we've won.

CHAMBERLAIN (*coming on*). Are you lost again ...

O'HALLORAN. No, no. There's someone there.
(MARGARET *has come on immediately behind the cart:*

26

she's followed by MOORE *who has to be helped by* JOAN.
MARGARET *goes back to draw him on.*)

CHAMBERLAIN. I can't see anything but the bloody wood.

LOGAN. His temper shortens by the hour.

O'HALLORAN. It does.

LOGAN. God: but we'll have a rest at least. (*Sinks down.*)
    (MORGAN *sinks down too.*)

PROCTOR. He's right, you know. There's someone there.

LOGAN. Go on: go on. I'll have a look. (*Looks round: other-
    wise he makes no gesture.*)

MOORE (*coming further on now, with* MARGARET's *and* JOAN's
    help). Are we lost again? Or do the paths divide?

JOAN. There's someone in the wood ahead.

MORGAN. They've marvellous eyes: I can't see a bloody thing
    meself ...

CHAMBERLAIN. It's nothing but the light ... Let's push ahead.

LOGAN. You go yourself: I'm sittin' here.

MARGARET. If there's someone there, why aren't they com-
    ing out?

O'HALLORAN. They're watching us ...

PROCTOR. They're making sure ...

LOGAN. They're counting up and then ... they'll pounce.

PROCTOR. There's one of them ... He's over there. (*Points
    off diagonally behind.*)

LOGAN. Good God: we're bloody done for now.

MORGAN. Why don't we run while we have a chance?

O'HALLORAN. There's another over there ...

LOGAN. And there.

MORGAN. I told you we shouldn't have stayed with these ...

PROCTOR. Too late to run: they're all around.

LOGAN. There's another one, you see — ahead.

    (*They draw together.* KENNEDY, *a soldier, comes on. He
    walks slowly round.*)

KENNEDY. What's this?

CROMWELL

O'HALLORAN. A box.

KENNEDY. And what's inside?

LOGAN. Come nearer and you'll begin to smell.

MOORE. It's the body of my brother.

MARGARET. We're taking it to a place of rest.

KENNEDY. And who are these?

MOORE. This is my brother's grandchild ... and this his daughter.

(BROOME, *a second soldier, comes on.*)

KENNEDY. And him? (*Indicating* MATHEW.)

MOORE. A servant of the house.

BROOME. And these?

JOAN. These are men from the village, who came to help.

BROOME. Five men: one cart?

(*Pause.*)

KENNEDY. What denomination are you, then?

O'HALLORAN. Protestant.

LOGAN. Oh, Protestant.

KENNEDY. I've never heard of a Protestant before ...

BROOME. Speaking with a Celtic tongue.

O'HALLORAN. Oh, thousands, thousands: all around.

BROOME. And you?

CHAMBERLAIN. I'm one of these.

BROOME. Five men to pull one cart.

O'HALLORAN. All volunteers.

BROOME. That's what I thought ... (*Examines cart: lifts handle. To* MOORE) An older, or a younger brother, then?

MOORE. Older ... Much older.

BROOME. And much lighter than yourself.

MOORE. He was.

BROOME. And yet the weight in here is like a ton of lead.

MARGARET. I've never felt the weight myself.

BROOME. Have you never touched the box?

MARGARET. Not since I saw him put inside.

BROOME. I think we'll have the lid up, then.

MARGARET. No!

JOAN. Never.

BROOME. We've seen this artifice before ... A man brought through our lines, with more than a thousand pounds upon his head.

LOGAN. To God... Is this what we've been let in for, then.

(*He starts to move:* KENNEDY *gestures him back.*)

MOORE (*approaching*). You mustn't touch that, sir. The man is dead.

BROOME. If it's as you say, you've nought to fear: the man's unburied, the rites unsaid ...

(*He prises back the lid: the relatives call out, thrust back by* KENNEDY *with his sword.* MATHEW *gestures round the cart.*)

What's this?

(MOORE *doesn't answer.*)

Your brother was a trooper, then?

MARGARET. What?

BROOME. Age thirty-four or five ...

MARGARET. What?

BROOME. And died from what?

MARGARET. Old age ...

BROOME. I'd say from a knife around his neck.

MARGARET. What's this?

BROOME. Lean over, woman ... You must have a look.

MARGARET. Oh, *God.*

JOAN. No.

BROOME (*to* MOORE). I see no surprise in you, old man.

LOGAN. Jesus, now, O'Halloran: but look at this.

O'HALLORAN. A man as big as a mountain we've been towing round all day.

KENNEDY. So this is what they've done.

BROOME. If you'd said a trooper, we might have let you pass

29

... But to hide a corpse away: it brings one thought to mind.

MARGARET (*to* MOORE). Tell him. Tell him. We've never seen this thing before ... Never. Not anywhere ... I swear to God ...These men! What have you done with him?

O'HALLORAN. To Jesus, now: we've never even looked.

LOGAN. You've slept beside the cart yourself.

O'HALLORAN. The stench an' all ...

LOGAN. 'A sacred smell': I've heard you use the words yourself.

PROCTOR. The nails have not been touched till now ...

MORGAN. This splintered wood is fresh.

O'HALLORAN. But no one's touched the box at all.

LOGAN. You see: we were on our way to market, sir ...

O'HALLORAN. That's right.

LOGAN. My friend and I: and this gentleman here was passing by ...

O'HALLORAN. Asked us if we'd give a lift.

LOGAN. The lady's tears—my God, your honour: you've never seen the like.

O'HALLORAN. Pouring down her cheeks, they were.

LOGAN. And one or two other places, now, besides.

O'HALLORAN. I've never seen so many tears.

LOGAN. No. No.

O'HALLORAN. Not since your mother died.

LOGAN. That's right.

BROOME. And so this corpse was invisibly transported, miraculously placed inside the wood and your aged, lightweight brother—if such a man existed which I doubt —with the same astonishing dexterity ... passed out.

MOORE. I've nothing to say.

MARGARET (*to* BROOME). My father died. I watched them place him in the box myself ... Joan ... Even Mathew ... he'd tell you if he could.

(MATHEW *nods, evidently agreeing, gesturing at the box.*)
What're you all silent for? ... Joan? ... Uncle?
(*Pause.*)
Have you seen this man before?
(MATHEW, *dancing round the cart, is nodding, pointing at the box.*)
What is he? ... Where's my father gone?

BROOME. Madam: these questions are no concern of mine. The evidence is plain to see: a murdered corpse, moving furtively between the lines: you'll come with us. We'll leave the body here ... These men can dig a grave.

O'HALLORAN What's that? What's that?

LOGAN. Not us?

O'HALLORAN. To Jesus, now, your honour ...

LOGAN. We've never seen the man before.

MORGAN. If we dig a grave, then, can we go?

BROOME. You'll break down branches ... Dig with that ... When the corpse is covered you'll come with us ...

O'HALLORAN. To God, then, Logan: what a mess.

MORGAN. Didn't I tell you we should never have stayed before.

LOGAN. Chamberlain, you know: you haven't said a word.

CHAMBERLAIN. There's no word to say: we do as the soldier says.
(*The men depart.*
MARGARET *has stepped back from the cart: she leans on* JOAN.
MOORE *stands immobilized by the cart:* MATHEW *still dances round it, gesturing.*
As the men move off PROCTOR *moves over to the women.*)

PROCTOR. There's nothing you can do now, you know ...
(*They make no response.*)
It's no good grieving: the dead are dead.

31

o'halloran. And so are we, my friend: this time tomorrer, I'm thinking ... We'll be looking for a box ourselves.
(*They move off.*
Light fades.)

Scene 7

The light comes up.

CHAMBERLAIN, O'HALLORAN, LOGAN, PROCTOR *and* MORGAN *are crouched together, linked by a rope.*

o'halloran. They don't take any prisoners here.
morgan. What's that?
o'halloran. Ask Chamberlain: he knows.
(CHAMBERLAIN *makes no answer.*)
o'halloran. They travel light.
logan. No excess baggage.
o'halloran. Take us out into the woods ... (*Makes a splitting sound.*)
logan. That's right.
chamberlain. I think we ought to agree on a single alibi while we have the chance.
logan. What alibi?
o'halloran. What chance?
chamberlain. That we were travelling away from the war.
morgan. Like refugees.
o'halloran. Five men, you mean ... ?
logan. Five stalwart men.
o'halloran. Five stalwart men, you mean, like us ... ?
logan. We could say we were going to enlist, you know ... On the Big One's side, that is, not ours.

O'HALLORAN. And we'll be bottled up in armour, then, as soon as not ...

LOGAN. Pushed out.

O'HALLORAN. Blown up.

LOGAN. Ones like us they put out first ...

O'HALLORAN. To see which way the shrapnel bursts ...

LOGAN. Fodder for the guns: he's right.

O'HALLORAN. Nevertheless, there, Logan ... It's our only chance.

PROCTOR. Can you shift your allegiance, then, as easily as that?

LOGAN. When there's a sword dangling by my throat I can shift it any way you like ... Come on ... come on: you can test it if you want.

CHAMBERLAIN. I think it's better that we act alike: we were moving from the war. It's up to them to prove us wrong.

MORGAN. Proof? What proof? They'll need no proof. A corpse like the one we had. One look at that: you could see his face. The verdict's spoken, man, before we step outside.

LOGAN. I can see that trooper's features right enough ... puffed up ... I thought he had a mouth, festering, beneath the opening where his real one stood: grinning, he was, from ear to ear, his head tossed back ...

PROCTOR. We've heard enough.

LOGAN. How they got him in I've no idea.

O'HALLORAN. Methinks I've seen the man before.

MORGAN. Before?

O'HALLORAN. Up here. (*He nods his head.*) The description of a tale I heard.

PROCTOR. Listen ...

CHAMBERLAIN. There's someone coming back ...

> (*They wait.*
> KENNEDY *hurls in* MOORE.)

KENNEDY. Get in, old fool: and wait with these ...

MORGAN. And are we likely to be getting out, then, soon?

O'HALLORAN. Out and into something worse.

(KENNEDY *fastens the old man to the rope.*)

PROCTOR. Where are the women, then?

KENNEDY. Out there.

PROCTOR. Waiting to be questioned, too?

(*A cry off.*)

O'HALLORAN. Not waiting long ...

LOGAN. And who's in next?

KENNEDY. The next I call ... And until I do ... From none of
you mun I hear a word.

MORGAN. What's happened to the madman, then?

(KENNEDY *looks back, doesn't answer: goes.*)

MOORE. The afflicted one: he got away ...

LOGAN. Away?

PROCTOR. He won't get far: they'll bring him back.

MORGAN. Did you tell them all you knew, then, man?

MOORE. I did. (*They look to him.*) Of you: I hardly said a
word: we met by the road, that's all. By chance.

MORGAN. The corpse: the corpse: didn't they ask you what
you knew of that?

MOORE. I told them.

MORGAN. Go on. Go on.

MOORE. I put it in the box myself ...

PROCTOR. Your niece—the woman—she never knew?

(MOORE *shakes his head.*)

O'HALLORAN. Nor Joan.

MOORE. Nor Joan ... we panicked when the troopers came.
My brother was already dead, the lid in place ... My
niece's daughter came—There was a trooper, already
dead, lying in the hedge beyond the yard ... Killed: I
could see that at a glance. If they found him there ... I took
him up: while the women were distracted, hiding food,

what few possessions my brother had, I put him in the box—I could think of nothing else—and put my brother back into his bed ... They searched the house: I took them to the rooms upstairs: my niece, from grief, remained below ... I explained the box, my brother's corpse ... They never thought to look inside ... All they wanted, you see, was loot ... and food ... They came back in force, took all we had ...

(*Another cry off.*)

You see ... (*He struggles.*) They believe she knows as well...

LOGAN. There's nothing you can do, old man.

(*Pause.*)

PROCTOR. Didn't you ever tell her ... All these days: hauling the cart? Didn't you tell her it was another man inside?

MOORE. I hadn't the heart ... Her mind was fastened on the priest ... Once that was done I knew she'd rest ... My brother I buried the night we left ... He lies there, now. She wouldn't have known ... I think her mind has turned. She's learned it all ... Belief, you see, was the only thing she had ...

O'HALLORAN. Who killed the trooper? Did you find that out?

MOORE (*shakes his head*). I thought it was the girl, at first ... But now. I know as little, or as much, as her ...

(*Another cry off.*)

If I could ease my hands of this I'd go outside ... I should have said I'd killed the man myself ... I never thought of it until they led me out ... I tried to shout ... I've no reason now to live ... (*Struggles.*) I could exonerate them all ... What's this!

(*Another cry off.*)

MORGAN (*pulled by the rope*). Leave off, old man. There's nothing you can do.

(*Pause.*)

CHAMBERLAIN. The best we can do, I think, is go our separate ways ... Each tell the tale he wants.

PROCTOR. And you?

CHAMBERLAIN. I've got no choice ... I'll tell them who I am.

PROCTOR. I can't sit here ... sit still ... If the lunatic gets out, then so can I.

O'HALLORAN. Aye ... A fool gets out ...

LOGAN. And he's a fool ...

O'HALLORAN. And we're damn fools, I'm thinking, waiting to be shot.

LOGAN. Here! (*Warns.*) There's someone coming now ...

CHAMBERLAIN. Keep still.

(*A pause.* MARGARET *and* JOAN *come in, separately, silent: heads bowed, dishevelled.*
KENNEDY *follows them in.*
JOAN *sinks down;* MARGARET *still stands, abstracted.*)

KENNEDY. You ... You've most to say: we'll see you first.

O'HALLORAN. Me? Me? But I've nothing left to add.

MORGAN. Take me, officer ... I'll go in first.

(KENNEDY *looks from one to the other: sees* MORGAN's *look.*)

KENNEDY. All right ... One by one—they'll scarcely mind.

(KENNEDY *releases* MORGAN: *they go.*)

LOGAN. I don't trust that Morgan ... the greasy bastard.

O'HALLORAN. I've half a mind he means to tell them first ... Put in a word, and beg them for release.

MOORE. Margaret ... Are you all right? I can scarcely see you, girl.

(MARGARET *makes no gesture.* JOAN, *after a while, looks up.*)

JOAN. I think ... my mother's mind has gone ... She started singing when they beat her worst.

MOORE. I should have thought. I should ... I could have said I killed the man.

36

JOAN. I said that too ... The one who caught us laughed. 'A girl like you?' he said. (*She looks across.*) They'd laugh at you ... 'A man', they'd say, 'as old as that?'

MOORE. I could have crept up ... I might have cut his throat behind.

JOAN. I said that, too ... Crept up on what? Across a hedge ... I told them how he lay ... 'Didn't any branches shake, or twigs or leaves, or was the man asleep, you think?' ... I said, 'Asleep.' ... 'Yet his pipe, a moment before, you said, was lit ... ' Even then, I might have lied ... (*She shakes her head.*) I can't go on. I've nothing left ... He offered me — the officer — to take me to his tent out there ...

O'HALLORAN. The next time he asks you'll have no choice.

JOAN. For that, he'd exonerate us both from blame. (*Indicates* MARGARET.)

MOORE. Then, God: while you've still got a chance, my child ... what's that in preference to your mother's life?

JOAN. And you ... you'd be the prisoner then they'd have ... while I lie there and listen to the shot ...

MOORE. There's no shooting at this old man that's not already done ...

JOAN. You did your best ... you thought it right ... But for the priest, it might have worked ... As for compounding one tragedy with two ... I'd rather join you in your grief than step aside ...

(*She comes over to* MOORE, *kneeling, embracing him.*)

LOGAN. They're back.

O'HALLORAN. What?

LOGAN. There's someone out there, beyond the lines.

PROCTOR. Not one of them.

O'HALLORAN. Not Morgan coming back?

PROCTOR. The fool.

LOGAN. What?

PROCTOR. The idiot.

O'HALLORAN. He's seen!

PROCTOR. No ... He's creeping by the track ...

LOGAN. What's that he's got?

O'HALLORAN. Between his teeth ...

LOGAN. A knife, bejasus ...

PROCTOR. You can see it in the light ...

O'HALLORAN. Aye, there lies the cause, I think, of our bloody, botched-up tale.

> (*They wait.*
>
> MATHEW *comes in, sinks down, looks back: then comes across. He gestures with the knife: smiles, gestures, moving round.*)

There lies your cut-throat ... if he only had a tongue to tell.

LOGAN. They'll find another trooper stretched out there, laughing through his throat, I think ...

O'HALLORAN. He did it for the best, I haven't a doubt.

LOGAN. Aye!

> (*He and* O'HALLORAN *laugh between themselves.*)

PROCTOR. Here ... Mathew ... *Mathew* ... Cut me free!

> (*Gestures with the rope.*
>
> MATHEW *dances round.*)

Cut me free ... !

LOGAN. Don't ask the man: he'll stick it in your head.

PROCTOR. Here ... Mathew ...

O'HALLORAN. Ask the girl.

PROCTOR. Tell him ... ask him ... cut me free.

JOAN. Mathew ... Let me have the knife.

LOGAN. He'll have your fingers off, at least ... Don't try and take the thing. Look out!

O'HALLORAN. He's got the glitter in his eye: God help the soldier boys he meets.

PROCTOR. There ... there ... just cut me free ...

JOAN. Cut it, Mat ... Just cut the rope for me ...

(*He cuts the rope.*
PROCTOR *gets up.*
MATHEW *dances back: he stops.*
They wait.)

PROCTOR. The knife ... and would you let me have the knife, then, Mat?

O'HALLORAN. He'll let you have it right enough ... Look out, then, man. Look out.

PROCTOR. Let's have a look, then, Mat ... Come on.

O'HALLORAN. Don't take the knife, for God's sake, man ...

LOGAN. If you're going, man, for God's sake go ...

PROCTOR. I'm going armed: I can't go as I am ... In the dark, with a knife, I stand a chance.

(*He dances at* MATHEW: *takes his arm. Much stronger, he wrenches free the knife.*)

LOGAN. Bejasus, Mr Chamberlain ... But there's a soldier for your fight ... If you'd known he was at your side would you have waited back for us?

PROCTOR. Chamberlain: shall I cut you free?

CHAMBERLAIN. You're better on your own: one stands a chance, but two, no chance at all.

PROCTOR. Just say the word.

CHAMBERLAIN. I can hardly move ... I've brought them here: I'll stay with these.

PROCTOR. O'Halloran?

O'HALLORAN. To God: but I stand more chance in here ... I've never been one to go scrumping through a wood.

PROCTOR. Logan?

LOGAN. I'm not a military man, myself ... (*To* O'HALLORAN) No. No. One glance, I think, would tell you that.

O'HALLORAN. One glance, I think, without a doubt.

PROCTOR. Old man?

(MOORE *shakes his head.*)

JOAN (*as she meets* PROCTOR's *glance, also shakes her head*).

39

You're better on your own … My mother I couldn't leave, at least.

PROCTOR (*indicating* MATHEW). I'll leave him here.
(*He fastens* MATHEW *to his place on the rope.*)
When they count the heads don't say a word.

CHAMBERLAIN. Where do you hope to make for, then?

PROCTOR. I'll find the enlistment place. That's what I came to do …

LOGAN. When you get to the place, you know …

PROCTOR. What's that?

LOGAN. And they have a list, you see … *Logan*.

O'HALLORAN. Tell them what occurred.

PROCTOR. I see.

O'HALLORAN. Tell them to put a line right through … O'Halloran, I think, you'll find there, too.

PROCTOR. I will … (*Looks round, determined.*) I'll go the way the fool came in.

CHAMBERLAIN. Good luck.

PROCTOR. Aye. I'll need it. (*Goes.*)
(*They watch, but for* MARGARET *and* MOORE, *and* MATHEW, *who struggles with the rope.*)

LOGAN. He's through.

O'HALLORAN. He's not.

LOGAN. He is.

O'HALLORAN. You're right.

LOGAN. My God.

O'HALLORAN. The bloody fool.

LOGAN. He is

O'HALLORAN. Shan't ever see his like.

LOGAN. No, no.

O'HALLORAN. A soldier, Chamberlain, through and through.

CHAMBERLAIN. I believe you're right.

LOGAN. Saw it when we met.

O'HALLORAN. One thought inside his head.

LOGAN. Just one.

O'HALLORAN. Leaves all the rest ...

LOGAN. Uncluttered.

O'HALLORAN. A man of action.

LOGAN. Every time.

CHAMBERLAIN (*still looking off*). He's gone into the darkness now ...
> (*Pause.*
> *They wait, gazing off.*
> *Silence.*)

MOORE. Margaret? Won't you sit down, girl?
> (JOAN *has moved to* MARGARET: *she takes her hand.*)

JOAN. Let's sit beside the rest ... There's nothing left to do.

MARGARET. They lie there now ... unblessed ... Two fathers dead ... two husbands, sons and brothers ...

O'HALLORAN. What church is it, that has to bless the dead?

LOGAN. Haven't they enough on their hands already without waitin' for a priest?

MARGARET. He'll not enter into paradise without a priest.

LOGAN. We better be finding one ourselves, I think ... I can hear the feller coming back. Look out.

O'HALLORAN. Keep that wriggling idiot in line: he'll have our one clear military genius caught before he's run a mile.

KENNEDY (*entering*). Stand up ... Stand up ... Up on your feet ... All of you ... You as well.
> (*He's followed in by* MORGAN, *then* BROOME.
> *They get up slowly:* MATHEW, *cowed, is last to rise.*)

BROOME. So you're the recruiting man they sent.

CHAMBERLAIN (*looks to* MORGAN. *Then:*) I am.

BROOME. And these the particular specimens you chose.

CHAMBERLAIN. They're chosen by their faith and nothing more.

BROOME. A soldier is a soldier—fate, not faith, casts him in the role he has ... Would a man like you not join our side?

CHAMBERLAIN. I would not.

BROOME. Not even unto death.

CHAMBERLAIN (*pauses*). Not even unto that.

    (BROOME *watches him: moves on.*)

BROOME. And you?

O'HALLORAN. Oh ... oh ... If you're looking for recruits, your honour ...

LOGAN. I've always got the colours muddled up ...

O'HALLORAN. It's the uniforms, you see ...

LOGAN. Which side is which ...

O'HALLORAN. Left or right ...

LOGAN. Facing front or facing back.

O'HALLORAN. I could never decide, you see, myself ...

LOGAN. Always needed someone like your honour, your gracious, worshipful honour, to do it for me.

O'HALLORAN. I'm sure, now, but this was the very spot we meant.

LOGAN. The one we aimed for all the time.

O'HALLORAN. Set on the track the day we left ... pointed in the wrong direction.

LOGAN. *This* is the place! I think you're right.

BROOME. And this?

KENNEDY. This isn't the man we left ... The rope's been cut!

O'HALLORAN. He dealt us a terrible blow ...

LOGAN. He did.

O'HALLORAN. He had a knife—would you believe it—all the time ...

LOGAN. When no one's looking ...

O'HALLORAN. Cuts the rope.

LOGAN. Captured this raving lunatic here ...

O'HALLORAN. Set him in his place.

LOGAN. And went.

KENNEDY. Guard! (*Goes off.*)

O'HALLORAN. Would we go with him?

LOGAN. Would we not.

O'HALLORAN. This is the army we intended all the time.

LOGAN. If the man had only thought.

O'HALLORAN. It might have been the one he wants himself.

BROOME. Is this the fool who ran off from the cart?

O'HALLORAN. It is ... And the one who did the crime at that.

LOGAN. Putting two and two together ...

O'HALLORAN. Not that we'd know the facts, you see ...

LOGAN. Your honour ...

O'HALLORAN. Your worshipful grace ...

LOGAN. More a matter of speculation ...

O'HALLORAN. Speculation ...

LOGAN. Speculation there, I think you're right.

KENNEDY (*returning*). They'll have him back ... He can't have travelled far.

BROOME. These two can serve us ... Cut them free. (*To* CHAMBERLAIN) And you, and the old man there, we'll bind afresh.

JOAN. No ... There's no need to bind a man as old as this.

BROOME. I think we have the culprit here ... I believe your mother's story, girl. Grief like that, I'm sure, is not pretence.

MOORE. It's true ... I killed him by the hedge.

JOAN. No.

MOORE. The girl: she found him ... nothing else.

JOAN. He could never kill a man! He can't!

(KENNEDY *starts to take him out.*)

MOORE. Joan ... it's better that I go like this ... Just think of me: I'm going gladly ... (*Goes to her.*) What other role could this poor body have. I've done with life.

BROOME. Take him out!

(KENNEDY *thrusts* MOORE *out.*)

As for you ... and your mother ... I shall set you free ...

The idiot too ... He can do no worse than jabber his silence in some other camp ... (*To* CHAMBERLAIN) And as for you: your head we'll carry through the villages on a pike and announce the end of one recruiting-drive with the beginning of another ... The old man's too we'll set up on a pike and travelling a little in advance allow it to proclaim the end of all men who might be tempted to take a trooper's life ... But as for now ... Three troops for one ...

LOGAN. That's right. Three. Three. That's quite correct.

BROOME. If Mr Morgan here will lead the way.

O'HALLORAN. Ah, a man with a level head at last.

(*Exit.*
Fade.)

ACT TWO

Scene 1

O'HALLORAN *and* LOGAN *enter, attired as soldiers.*

O'HALLORAN. You see, you see, now: lost again.
LOGAN. I'm sure this is the path we should have taken.
O'HALLORAN. If only armies would stand like men ... put out two fists, you know, and fight ... all these furtive shifts about ...
LOGAN. Two hours ago I could have told you where I was.
O'HALLORAN. Outflank them to the left, he said.
LOGAN. Ah, now ... Are you sure it wasn't the right?
O'HALLORAN. Right or left ... at no time in the centre where it counts.
LOGAN. In the centre, of course, he stands himself.
O'HALLORAN. While all goes on to left and right ...
LOGAN. And where the armies should have met ...
O'HALLORAN. Stands no one but himself ...
LOGAN. And the other chief, of course.
O'HALLORAN. That's right.
LOGAN. The best thing we can do ... (*Sits down.*)
O'HALLORAN. You're right ... (*Lies down.*)
     (*Sounds of cannon off.*)
LOGAN. Ah, to God: they chose a day.
O'HALLORAN. They did.
LOGAN. Not a breath o' wind ...
O'HALLORAN. Not a drop o' cloud.
     (*They stretch out.*)
LOGAN. If I could get this off I think I'd bathe.
O'HALLORAN. If I thought I could get it on again.
LOGAN. The logic, you see, of being trussed up.

45

(*Cannon off.*)

Was that a bird?

O'HALLORAN. I think it was.

LOGAN. The noise beyond ...

O'HALLORAN. Obliterates the sound.

LOGAN. At least one thing ...

O'HALLORAN. Three meals a day.

LOGAN. Three meals a day and a drop to drink.

O'HALLORAN. A roof above your head at times.

(*Cannon off.*)

O'HALLORAN. Jasus: if they'd turn that off. (*Yawns, stretches, lying back.*)

LOGAN. A day like this, I wouldn't mind ...

O'HALLORAN. No, no ...

LOGAN. Making the effort ...

O'HALLORAN. That's right ...

LOGAN. To stay alive. (*Yawns hugely: settles back.*)

(*They doze.*

Pause.

MORGAN *enters, similarly attired, a superior rank.*)

MORGAN. And what the hell's going on down here?

LOGAN. To God ... It's the commander-in-chief himself.

O'HALLORAN. To Jesus, Morgan ... but you made me start.

MORGAN. You're supposed to outflank the place, not stretch out on the ground.

O'HALLORAN. Now would that be to the left, or right?

MORGAN. The right ...

LOGAN. That's where, you see, we went astray.

O'HALLORAN. I told him to the left.

LOGAN. No, no ... *I* to the left ... I believe you said the right.

O'HALLORAN. No, no ... I to the left, I believe and Logan to the right.

LOGAN. Nevertheless, I'll take the blame.

O'HALLORAN. No, no, but I'll take it on myself. I shall.

MORGAN. Whatever the way, you'll follow me. Pick up
    your weapons ... Get up off the ground.

LOGAN. Oh, dear ...

O'HALLORAN. Oh, my.

LOGAN. No sooner settled down.

    (*They start to rise.*)

O'HALLORAN. A pitiless man.

LOGAN. He is at that.

O'HALLORAN. Where's the Morgan we used to know ...

LOGAN. Beneath those superannuated stripes.

    (PROCTOR *comes in, attired as one of the opposing forces.*)

PROCTOR. Stand fast ...

O'HALLORAN. To God ... An enemy at last.

LOGAN. And fierce, to boot.

O'HALLORAN. And fierce, at that.

MORGAN. Put down your arms: you're outnumbered three
    to one.

PROCTOR. Outnumbered, but not outfought: do you think
    I give a damn!

LOGAN. Proctor, to God! 'Tis the blacksmith man himself.

O'HALLORAN. See ... your friends: you've found your
    friends at last.

PROCTOR. No friends of mine in rags like that.

LOGAN. Oh, God: another monomanic fool ...

O'HALLORAN. See ... see ... beneath this mask ...

LOGAN. O'Halloran ...

O'HALLORAN. Logan.

PROCTOR. I recognize you well enough.

O'HALLORAN. And Morgan.

PROCTOR. And Morgan ...

LOGAN. Promoted ... Oh, promoted above the heads of
    O'Halloran and me.

PROCTOR. Lay down your arms, or strike at that.

O'HALLORAN. To God, but we'd hardly touch a friend ...

LOGAN. Or foe.

(O'HALLORAN *and* LOGAN *toss down their arms.*)

PROCTOR. Allegiance, I see ... like the coat upon your back ... tossed on or off, according to the cloud or light.

O'HALLORAN. Oh, we have a great interest ...

LOGAN. In seeing the rights and wrongs ...

O'HALLORAN. Of every side.

LOGAN. There are two sides at least to every question.

O'HALLORAN. Three or four, if the truth were known.

LOGAN. Only a fool would come down on one.

O'HALLORAN. While a real man at least comes down on two.

PROCTOR. Morgan has gone too far to change his suit ... it's veritably fastened round his neck with braid ... each stripe a stroke of treason to our cause ... Well, Morgan: let's see your sword unravel that. (*Puts up his sword.*)

(*They fight.*

Cannons rumble off.)

LOGAN. Ah, now ... oh, now ...

O'HALLORAN. Oh, dear ... oh, dear ...

LOGAN. Don't take it seriously, now ...

O'HALLORAN. 'Tis only war.

(LOGAN *and* O'HALLORAN *dance out of the way: they alternatively cover their eyes and watch.*)

LOGAN. Oh, dear ... oh, dear ...

O'HALLORAN. But what a sight.

LOGAN. Friends: remember ... men beneath the shirt.

PROCTOR. No man is this ... A rat, and turncoat. Nothing else.

MORGAN. And this an ass: allegiance fastened like a shroud around his head.

PROCTOR. 'Tis a flag of honour you see, my friend.

MORGAN. 'Tis a blindfold, masking common sense.

o'halloran. All this, all this: and poetry too!
(morgan *and* proctor *fight on.*)

logan. 'Tis a mystifying thing is war.

o'halloran. Once killed, you know, there's nothing else.

proctor. I'd rather die like this than linger in a bed ... or switch my side for advancement o'er my friends.
(*They fight with shouts and groans.*)

logan. Idealists and opportunists.

o'halloran. We must hold aloof.
(morgan *falls:* proctor *stands over him with a sword.*)

proctor. Do you yield, then, Morgan ... traitor ... rat ... Or shall I pass this through you to the ground?

morgan. I yield. I yield.

logan. A sensible man, at last.
(*As* morgan *rises he tries to strike* proctor *down.*)

o'halloran. To God and Jesus, man: look out!
(proctor *turns: runs* morgan *through.*)

proctor. Traitors never learn until their crime is past.
(*Sheathes his sword.*)

logan. Your honour, then ...

o'halloran. We better find our path. (*Retreating.*)

logan. Through the forest wend our way ...

o'halloran. Weaponless ...

logan. Bereft of arms.

proctor. You'll come with me.

o'halloran. But shouldn't we trot off home ... You, me, Logan: the three of us are nothing but village-men at heart ... This war ...
(*Cannon roar.*)
We had a part ...

logan. The role's expired.

o'halloran. There's nothing left ...

LOGAN. We could excuse ourselves ...

O'HALLORAN. Retire ...

LOGAN. No one the wiser ...

O'HALLORAN. Nor better off.

LOGAN. Nor worse.

PROCTOR. If everyone thought like you there'd be no war ... No principle, honour, virtue ... no cause to raise a man at all.

LOGAN. Ah, but many to celebrate its absence with.

O'HALLORAN. Unmaimed.

LOGAN. Unkilled.

O'HALLORAN. Unblinded.

LOGAN. Take Morgan here ...

O'HALLORAN. Three stripes.

LOGAN. A little longer he might have counted more ... while here, you see ... (*Indicating his own arm.*) No mark at all.

PROCTOR. I see no principle of any sort in that.

LOGAN. Principle, you see, is like a cart: jump on, jump off ... Poor Morgan fell between ... while we: the slightest commotion knocks us off ... no principle, you see, can hold us long ... no principle, for instance, Proctor, leaves its mark ...

PROCTOR. The principle of self-preservation, I imagine: nothing else.

LOGAN. What's preserved of Morgan, now, but these? ... the stripes, the boots, the sword ... a rag to hand on now to someone else ... some deluded, animated corpse— waves them in the air and screams, dying or dismembered or blinded, for a cause ... And when one cause expires but its opposite begins ... Proctor's flag today ... tomorrow ... this.

PROCTOR. You'll come with me ... without ideals no man can live.

LOGAN. And with ideals we end like this. (*Gestures round.*)
(*They go.*
Light fades.)

Scene 2

Light comes up.

PROCTOR *comes on, tired, his uniform loosened: still authoritative, stern.*

He's followed by O'HALLORAN *and* LOGAN: *they've discarded their uniform to varying degrees.*

O'HALLORAN. The battle's like a carrot to the man ... the faster he goes, the quicker it passes on.

PROCTOR. It's a rout ... one side has fled—the other's given chase.

LOGAN. On horse, or machines, I'd say: but not on foot ... (*Sits.*) Dispose of us both, then, Proctor ... I'll not move another step from here.

O'HALLORAN (*sinks down*). To God, a military boot is that: a hole big enough to let another foot stick out.

PROCTOR. There's a farmhouse over there. We'll make for that.

O'HALLORAN. You'll have to carry him ... and me.

PROCTOR. I'll reconnoitre it ... Do you give your word you'll stay?

LOGAN. I'll stay.

O'HALLORAN. I'll stay ... I'll stay beside my feet at least ... and where my feet are now ... I'll rest.

LOGAN. Go on then, feller, for we'll never leave.
(PROCTOR *goes.*)

O'HALLORAN. 'Tis a dishevelled bloody place at that.

LOGAN. No roof.

51

O'HALLORAN. Two walls ...

LOGAN. The other two removed.

O'HALLORAN. A damn great bomb, I think, has tumbled down the thatch.

LOGAN. To God ... (*He stretches out.*)

O'HALLORAN. Hauled between armies ...

LOGAN. Like fish inside a net.

O'HALLORAN. 'Tis a disagreeable business, war ... when one side wins, the other breaks its neck ... To God ... but don't look now ... That ijit's back ... the one we knew before.

(MATHEW *has come on, dishevelled, carrying a long, thin loaf.*)

LOGAN. Has he got a knife?

O'HALLORAN. A sword.

LOGAN. Holy Mother ... Captured by a madman now!

O'HALLORAN. I think he's smiled ...

LOGAN. Or grinned ...

O'HALLORAN. I can't be sure ... Your honour ... don't you remember us, your grace ... To Jasus, Logan: but he's coming up.

LOGAN. And where's the Captain now? ... About to lose two prisoners and he's vanished out of sight ... (*Calls*) Proctor!

O'HALLORAN. Proctor!

LOGAN. No, no ... it is a smile, you're right.

O'HALLORAN. What I thought was a sword is a loaf of bread.

LOGAN. Food ... but, Jesus: what a sight.

(*They've got up hastily.*

MATHEW, *nodding and grinning, offers the loaf.*)

O'Halloran, I must be dreaming yet ...

O'HALLORAN. Tell me if I'm wrong ...

LOGAN. Isn't that the girl herself?

(JOAN *enters, followed by* PROCTOR. *She carries a pitcher of water.*)

JOAN. I've brought you this: water, I'm afraid: we've nothing else.

(*They take the pitcher as greedily as they've taken the bread.*)

O'HALLORAN. To God: but that's the loveliest stuff on earth. (*Drinks.*)

JOAN. I sent Mat out: the soldiers came ... the bread was all we had to hide.

PROCTOR. The soldiers ... were their coats ... like theirs ... or mine?

JOAN. Like yours ... or theirs ... They look alike.

PROCTOR. Woman. This coat is different from the rest!

LOGAN. Do you want a drink? Or do we throw the rest away?

(PROCTOR *hesitates, then takes it.*)

O'HALLORAN. Do you want the bread, or not?

(PROCTOR *takes it.*)

JOAN. The battle's gone ... the soldiers went away ... the fields are burnt ... the house is down.

LOGAN (*indicating* PROCTOR). New principles, I can see, must be fashioned now.

O'HALLORAN. The war has gone ...

LOGAN. And left its principal behind.

O'HALLORAN. I can see the fellers now ...

LOGAN. 'And where's the man with all the stripes?'

O'HALLORAN. 'Proctor was the name.'

LOGAN. 'Fell on the field ... or deserted, sir.'

O'HALLORAN. Which is all the same when the fighting's done.

LOGAN. When the fighting's o'er, and the battle won.

(O'HALLORAN *and* LOGAN *laugh:* PROCTOR *stands as if immobilized.*)

O'HALLORAN. And you, young lady: is your mother well?

LOGAN. Better off than she was before?

JOAN. She died—the night we left the camp ... I think her brain was seized ... we brought her on the cart ... she lies out there ... beside her father now ...

53 ·

(*They pause.*

PROCTOR *removes his cap: sits down.*)

LOGAN. And now the sword.

O'HALLORAN. Without his principles, you mean ... he might bend the path.

LOGAN. Divert it, as it were, from its original course.

PROCTOR (*to* JOAN). Will you stay here?

JOAN. We can come with you.

PROCTOR. We'll find a place where no one fights ... with words, with ideas, with philosophies ... but not with these. (*Kicks his sword aside.*)

LOGAN. One madness exits but to greet the next.

PROCTOR. We'll go that way ... yonder ... where the wood's untouched ... We'll find a place where we can rest a while ... I'm tired. I've had enough of war ... We'll find a place for moral argument.

(*They go:* PROCTOR *leading, followed by* JOAN *and* MATHEW.

LOGAN *and* O'HALLORAN *follow last.*

Light fades.)

Scene 3

Light comes up: muted.

They enter.

JOAN. I think the wood grows thicker here ...

LOGAN. The path, I see, is fadin' too.

PROCTOR. From the top of the hill the way seemed clear.

O'HALLORAN (*coming in last*). Clear from above, but muddled once below.

(*A wild figure leaps in: a huge shriek: it whirls a sword.*

Long-haired, almost naked, CLEET *flashes his sword before
   them.*)

CLEET. Stand fast, you slimy bastards! ... Did you think I'd
   let you through!

O'HALLORAN. Through?

LOGAN. Through what, your honour?

CLEET. Through woods I call my own.

O'HALLORAN. We were not aware ...

LOGAN. We were distinctly unaware ...

O'HALLORAN. That these beautiful trees ...

LOGAN. Were all your own.

   (CLEET *flourishes his sword more wildly still: he leaps
   round them with fresh impetus.*)

O'HALLORAN. We thought, that is ...

LOGAN. They belonged to the Big One, then.

CLEET. The Big One, did you?

O'HALLORAN. The one who ... won the war.

LOGAN. That's right.

   (CLEET *seems less disposed towards them now than ever.*
   O'HALLORAN *and* LOGAN *glance at one another.*)

O'HALLORAN. The one, of course ... to whom we're indisposed.

CLEET. Indisposed to the Big One, are ye?

LOGAN. The one who won the war?

CLEET. That's right. (*He waits.*)

O'HALLORAN. If he's the One ...

LOGAN. We think he is ...

O'HALLORAN. He's the One to whom ...

LOGAN. With whom ...

O'HALLORAN. For whom ...

CLEET. You're on the Big One's side, or mine?

LOGAN. Oh, definitely ...

O'HALLORAN. Yours, your honour ...

LOGAN. Your grace ...

O'HALLORAN. Your worship ...

LOGAN. Every time.

CLEET. And these?

O'HALLORAN. Oh, these are friends of ours ...

LOGAN. Of his ...

O'HALLORAN. Of yours.

LOGAN. Of mine.

CLEET. I'll take you to our camp-place, then. My name is
   Cleet. One word of where we go, of how we get there,
   of what it looks like once we're fast inside ...

O'HALLORAN. Oh, now ... not a word.

LOGAN. Not a murmur.

O'HALLORAN. Not a sound.

LOGAN. Shan't say a thing.

O'HALLORAN. To God, your honour ...

LOGAN. You can trust us ...

O'HALLORAN. Every time.

   (CLEET *turns to lead the way.*)

   To God and Jesus, now: what's this: a madman clears the
   field apace; where thistles, grass and nettle grew a second
   madman plants the weeds anew.

   (*They go.*
   Light fades.)

Scene 4

Light comes up.
   They're sitting in a circle.
   In addition to CLEET *there are two other wild and heavily-armed*
figures: WALLACE *and* DRAKE.

CLEET. These are my comrades you can see gathered here.

LOGAN. Armed for a resurrection ...

56

o'halloran. Insurrection ...

logan. Insurrection ... I can see that at a glance.

wallace. The woods on either side are filled with men.

drake. And beside each man ...

wallace. A sword.

drake. A gun.

o'halloran. And these are against the Big One, too?

wallace. The one who took the land.

o'halloran. And when the Big One's beaten, then?

drake. You'll see a place where everything is shared.

wallace. No land, no property, not common to us all.

logan. But when the insurrection starts ...

o'halloran. With the ones, you see, you've dispossessed ...

cleet. We'll stamp them out.

drake. A flame like ours is always lit.

wallace. Who's heard of the thing that can extinguish it?

o'halloran. To Jesus: but manic fools unite ...

logan. The better to prolong the fight.

cleet. Are you with us, then? (*Rises: sword drawn, stands over them.*) Or are you set against?

proctor. I'm tired of war ... We travelled to a place, I thought, where men took sides with words, not swords.

wallace. There is no such place.

drake. No words stake out their claim but swords are not drawn up behind.

joan. Yet if we don't ... Or if we can't.

wallace. No don't, or can't.

joan. Yet take up neither side ...

proctor. But stand aloof ...

joan. Looking to our own and nothing else.

cleet. Your own is ours ... and ours is yours to share.

drake. Our side, or theirs. (*Draws out his sword too.*)

proctor. We fall between the two ...

   (*Vast explosions on either side.*)

57

CLEET. To arms! The troops have reached the woods!
　　(*Other explosions.*)
　　To the trees! To the trees, God damn you! No prisoners,
　　now! We fight them to the end!
　　(*The three figures rush off in separate directions: cannon,
　　firing off.*)
O'HALLORAN. To Jesus, now ...
LOGAN. Come on ...
JOAN. Let's fly ...
O'HALLORAN. Proctor ... are you going to join the men?
JOAN. With us ... For God's sake, Proctor, fly!
　　(*They dash off, separately*.)
　　Mathew! ... This way ... Mathew! With us!
　　(*Fade.*)

Scene 5

Light comes up.
　　PROCTOR *and* JOAN *rest on the ground.*
　　MATHEW *is making a fire, cooking, some distance off.*

JOAN. Has he prepared the food?
PROCTOR. It won't be long.
JOAN. Are we safe this far away?
PROCTOR. We'll journey on.
JOAN. Or back.
PROCTOR. Or back?
JOAN. To the farm ... there's nowhere else ... You could
　　build a smithy: we could start again.
PROCTOR. Rebuild the place?
JOAN. Re-sow the fields ... build up the hedges ... repair the
　　thatch ... fashion walls.

PROCTOR. And have a child?

JOAN. That too.

(*Pause.*)

PROCTOR. It's hard ... (*He moves aside.*) I'm used to having
conviction on my side ... badges, stripes, emblems, that
tell me who and what and where I am ... To live like this
... (*He shakes his head.*) Subversionists and spies.

JOAN. Or lovers, who would have no thought ...

PROCTOR. But for themselves.

JOAN. What lover, in loving, does not love others too.

PROCTOR. Aye ...

(*She holds him.*
MATHEW *crosses with food: hesitates; retreats.*
Light fades.)

Scene 6

Light comes up.
A BOATMAN *who poles his boat across a river, now standing
on the bank.*
LOGAN *and* O'HALLORAN *enter.*

LOGAN. To God, but running wears me down ... surrender,
I think'd be an altogether less demanding thing.

O'HALLORAN. Bone, and a minimum of bone, and skin ...

LOGAN. And that's an optimum account.

O'HALLORAN. To God, and all that water too ...

BOATMAN. Are you the ones that passed through here before?

O'HALLORAN. Reduced in number now, you see.

BOATMAN. What happened to your companions? The girl?

LOGAN. The girl has gone.

O'HALLORAN. The blacksmith too.

LOGAN. Escorted by the madman.

BOATMAN. The rest?

O'HALLORAN. Are dead.

BOATMAN. The mother, too?

LOGAN. If we told the tale, it would never end.

BOATMAN (*shakes his head*). Many the men who cross this stream ... and many the history they have to tell ... the world's abuse, the world's acclaim ... they set their paths by distant lights ... while I, day in, day out, navigate between two shadowy shores ...

O'HALLORAN. Oh, indispensable, despite the tedium of the task.

BOATMAN. And overlooked ... the use is all: without the boat they're lost.

LOGAN. A boat, I can see, we shall have to build ourselves.

O'HALLORAN. Or swim.

BOATMAN. Too deep: too fast.

LOGAN. And men like us?

BOATMAN. Without the price no man can pass.

LOGAN. To God, O'Halloran ... A job.

O'HALLORAN. And here I'd been thinking we might last without.

LOGAN. We'll travel back.

O'HALLORAN. A soldier's pay.

LOGAN. A labourer's hire.

O'HALLORAN. When we've got the price ...

LOGAN. We'll cross the stream.

BOATMAN. When that day comes—you'll find me here.
    (*They turn away.*)

LOGAN. I had a dream.

O'HALLORAN. Ah, yes.

LOGAN. I heard a choir ...

O'HALLORAN. Singing.

LOGAN. Very loud and clear.

O'HALLORAN. And when the singing stopped ...
LOGAN. A bird.
O'HALLORAN. And when you looked?
LOGAN. I saw it perched.
O'HALLORAN. The topmost branch ...
LOGAN. Of a nearby tree ...
    You've heard this dream before, I think.
O'HALLORAN. I have.
LOGAN. No need to tell you how it ends.
    (*They go.*
    BOATMAN *waits.*
    Stage darkens.)

ACT THREE

Scene 1

JOAN *enters.*
   PROCTOR *with a scythe.*

PROCTOR. How's the child?

JOAN. She's fine ... See ...

PROCTOR. Running in the fields.

JOAN. The country's quiet.

PROCTOR. The crops swell out the barn ... The tenancy is
   paid.

JOAN. The smithy crackles with its stove all day.

PROCTOR. The dead: familiar ghosts ...

JOAN. Not demons, screaming in the mind.

PROCTOR. The house filled out with children's cries.

JOAN. And here two labourers, worthy of their hire.
   (*They laugh.*
      O'HALLORAN *and* LOGAN *come on.*)

O'HALLORAN. Good evening, your honour.

LOGAN. Missis ... It's a lovely night.

PROCTOR. Are you going far — or home to bed?

LOGAN. We're travelling, let me see ...

O'HALLORAN. To the nearest bar.

JOAN. And savings ... that you came to make?

LOGAN. Saved for the day ...

O'HALLORAN. But spent throughout the night.

PROCTOR. We'll see you in the morning, then?

LOGAN. Aye. God willing.

O'HALLORAN. If the sun hangs right.
   (*They go.*)

JOAN. Stars.

PROCTOR. And moon.

JOAN. Shaped like a scythe.

PROCTOR. A sickle: angled at the chimney, then ... (*Looks round after a while.*) I'll call the child.

JOAN. Time to retire ... I'll set the table.

PROCTOR. Bolt the door.

JOAN. And settle in our haven, then.
    (*They go.*
    Light fades.)

Scene 2

Light comes up.
    CLEET, *bloodied, bandaged, helped by* WALLACE. DRAKE *has come ahead.*

DRAKE. Here's a place.

WALLACE. We'll hide in here.

DRAKE. Warm and dry.

CLEET. A barn ... I can scarcely see.
    (*They ease him down.*)

WALLACE. The troopers ...

CLEET. Are they far behind?

DRAKE. Not far.

WALLACE. They'll never search in here.

CLEET. There's someone here! ... Listen ...
    (*Points blindly.*
        MATHEW *rises from where he's been asleep.*)
    Who is it?

WALLACE. An idiot, going by his stare.

DRAKE. He's armed.

WALLACE. A knife.

63

CLEET. Disarm him, then ...

(DRAKE *and* WALLACE *advance on* MATHEW. *He turns and runs.*)

WALLACE. He's gone.

CLEET. Quick ... outside!

DRAKE. He'll not get far ... I'll take him in the night.

(*He goes.*

CLEET *lies back.*)

CLEET. That battle ... Wallace? I thought we'd see them run.

WALLACE. We did.

CLEET. Aye ... And turn ... in greater number still.

WALLACE. Set-pieces are not the way to fight ... out on the plain, in open fields ...

CLEET. We can't live in the woodland all our lives: I thought the time had come ... we'd see men rise, flock round us ... As it is ... they work and sleep ... think little ... feel nothing ... the profit of their work drawn off ... quiescent ... dreamers ... full of beer and bread ...

WALLACE. What's that?

(*Draws his sword, rising.*

PROCTOR *has entered. He's followed in by* MATHEW.)

PROCTOR. This is my barn ... Without my permission you've no rights in here.

WALLACE. Our barn ... This is our barn ...

CLEET. I must commend you on the way it's kept.

WALLACE. Well-stocked ...

CLEET. And warm.

WALLACE. The roof well thatched.

PROCTOR. By my labour ... and by my effort ... By that of no one else.

CLEET. We had other work to do.

PROCTOR. Aye. I see.

CLEET. Which inflicts a heavier price than the one you're at.

PROCTOR. Not a price I asked, or set.

CLEET. But all would set the price who hold things to themselves.

PROCTOR. The things I've worked for I've fashioned by myself ...

CLEET. And family?

PROCTOR. For my wife and child.

(DRAKE *comes in.*)

DRAKE. I followed him in here ... I see he's fetched his master out.

WALLACE. This man, I think, we've met before.

DRAKE. The one who's sick of war: you're right.

WALLACE. He sets his sword aside ... and ploughs ... sets up his little household here ...

DRAKE. And thinks the world outside has died.

CLEET. There are men outside who have no land to till ... no crops to grow ... no wife to feed ... no child, no house, no barn ... no bread ... no wine ... no place to call their own. You have no answer, I can see, to that.

PROCTOR. What do you want of me? ... I'd rather join that throng than fight again.

CLEET. And would a brave man play that part?

PROCTOR (*approaches*). A brave man makes his life. He saves it if he can ... Do you think one bloodied head ... a thousand heads ... a mile of corpses ... will change by one degree the world out there?

WALLACE. The man's insane.

CLEET (*to* PROCTOR). The world stands still ...

PROCTOR. As the top parts grow ... so do the branches underneath ... A tree bears up its leaves ... hoists up its branches ... and grows by the reaching out of its extremities to the sun and sky ... You—you would have us like a hedge ... hacked down each year to a common height.

WALLACE. The man is mad.

CLEET. And of oppression?

PROCTOR. One awards each man according to his need ... change by degree ... a dead man is no longer fit for good or ill: a live man, however hard, can be fashioned by his will.

CLEET. And of those oppressed so hard that nature stops their growth?

PROCTOR. I see no oppression harder than the one you bring in here ... is life perfected by the loss of blood? What world was made that wasn't unmade for its good?

DRAKE. We have another philosopher, Cleet, I see.

CLEET. Who casts his eye so far it overlooks our heads.

PROCTOR. My eyes are cast about my feet — my hands, the soil, my wife, my child ... my true barter with people of like mind. My toil, my labour ... I carry revolution in my head, and heart ... not streaked along a sword, or buried with the dead.

WALLACE. 'Tis cry and cry alike ... the cry for equality is the loudest cry of all ... Not for your barn, your labour, or your farm ... but for the goodness that lends them to us all.

PROCTOR. Have the barn ... What's broken down by you I can build again.

CLEET. Aye ... 'tis destruction you see in me ... and not the promotion of a higher cause.

PROCTOR. One thing I've found of causes ...

CLEET. Aye?

PROCTOR. No cause is greater than its means.

CLEET. Oppressors are met by oppressor's schemes.

PROCTOR. Then oppression makes reflections of itself — and calls it revolution ... change ... the end to discontent ... And change it is ... the beggar usurps the horseman and takes the whip himself.

(CLEET *turns aside*.)

CLEET. All I have need of now is rest ...

PROCTOR. Well, rest I'll not deny ... nor food ... Mathew: go to the house ... water ... and ointment to set a wound.
(MATHEW *goes.*
PROCTOR *kneels to look at* CLEET's *wound.*)
Aye ... it's bad enough ... The flesh has healed ... but the wound's begun to rot.

DRAKE. Do you think the man will die?

PROCTOR. It'll take a deeper thrust than that ... My wife can set the wound.

WALLACE. And after that?

PROCTOR. Ten days ... a week...

CLEET. We'll rest up here.

DRAKE. And for your services ...

PROCTOR. No services are those that meet a need.
(*Light fades.*)

Scene 3

Light comes up.
BROOME *enters: military figure, followed by* KENNEDY.

BROOME. Aye ... This is the place ... the track leads here.

JOAN (*enters*). Is there any way I can help you, sir?

KENNEDY. Aye ... we're looking for a troop of men.

BROOME. One wounded, if not two at least.

JOAN. What kind of men?

KENNEDY. Insurrectionists ...

BROOME. Subversionists ...

KENNEDY (*coming forward*). Anarchists: revolutionaries— men of simple mind.

JOAN. How do they appear?

BROOME. They wear no uniform of any kind.

JOAN. How does one describe them, then?

KENNEDY. They have no appearance, Ma'am, but simplicity itself ...

BROOME. Dirt ... and a general air of infestation.

KENNEDY. Evasiveness of manner ...

BROOME. And the inability to look one directly in the eye.
    (O'HALLORAN *and* LOGAN *enter.*)

O'HALLORAN. Good day, your honour.

LOGAN. Good day, your worship.

KENNEDY. Good day, yourself.

BROOME. Not these at least.

LOGAN. To God: but those are beautiful clothes you wear.

KENNEDY. The same's for you, if you want to join.

O'HALLORAN. Oh, but we're well contented to work down here.

LOGAN. With no disrespect to yourself, that is.

BROOME. We're looking for a troop of men.

JOAN. The only men we have are these ... The idiot yonder ... and my husband in the fields.

KENNEDY. Your husband's being brought in, I see.

BROOME. The men have encircled the place: there's no retreat.

O'HALLORAN. To God ...

LOGAN. Another war sprung up!

KENNEDY. What evidence have you found there, men?
    (*Two Soldiers enter with* PROCTOR.)

FIRST SOLDIER. Straw ...

SECOND SOLDIER. Stained with blood.

FIRST SOLDIER. And dressings, sir ...

SECOND SOLDIER. The sign of habitation in the barn.

KENNEDY. A hide-out, then.

O'HALLORAN. To God, your honour.

LOGAN. This is news to us.

BROOME (*to* JOAN). Haven't I seen your face before?

JOAN. You have.

KENNEDY (*to* PROCTOR). And yours too I thought I knew.

BROOME. And these ...

KENNEDY. There's a familiar ring about the place ... Sergeant: tighten the cordon. Break the hedge ... Set fire to the barn ... the house.

JOAN. No!

PROCTOR. No!

O'HALLORAN. To Jesus: but we've just built up the place ...

BROOME. Sheltering insurrectionists is a Federal crime ... your house is forfeit; your land as well ... Corporal, take these men in charge ...

JOAN. I have a child ... For God's sake: let me at the house!

KENNEDY. The house is fired.

LOGAN. The flame leaps up the thatch ...

PROCTOR. But let me near ... let me in the house!

(*The Soldiers hold him and* JOAN *back as they call out and scream.*)

JOAN. Oh, Jesus ... O my child ... if you have any pity left!

BROOME. Set light to the fields: we'll have these felons out ... no food or shelter: retreat turned into rout.

(*The light fades.*)

Scene 4

The light comes up.

JOAN, PROCTOR, *stooped, broken,* O'HALLORAN *and* LOGAN, *followed by* MATHEW, *form a line of figures that moves across the stage.*

Soldiers guard them on either side.

O'HALLORAN. Where are we bound to, Captain?

FIRST SOLDIER. Corporal.

LOGAN. But you have the face ...

O'HALLORAN. And bearing ...

LOGAN. Of a more distinguished man, your grace.

SECOND SOLDIER. We're taking you where you'll cause no trouble.

LOGAN (*to* O'HALLORAN). As safe as where we were before.

O'HALLORAN. Houses, are there?

FIRST SOLDIER. Aye.

LOGAN. And fields?

SECOND SOLDIER. Aye. A place to work for sure.
(*The Soldiers laugh.*)

O'HALLORAN. To God: we had enough of that before.

LOGAN. Are there many people there like us, your grace?

FIRST SOLDIER. Aye, Don't worry ... (*Laughs.*)

SECOND SOLDIER. You'll find there many more.
(*The Soldiers laugh.*
WALLACE *leaps on.*)

WALLACE. Lay down your arms! Stand back!
(*He's heavily armed: whirls sword.*)

O'HALLORAN. To Jesus: but we're overcome!
(DRAKE, *similarly attired, darts on: he stabs the Second Soldier as he draws his sword.*
He leaps to the First Soldier and with WALLACE, *runs him through.*)

LOGAN. But God and Holy Mary: they never gave the man a chance.

DRAKE. Do you come with us ... or join him there?

WALLACE. No time for half-decisions now.

O'HALLORAN. Aye ...

LOGAN. We're with you ...

O'HALLORAN. Always was.

PROCTOR. I'll choose the sword.

JOAN. He doesn't know his mind ... He'll go with you.

(JOAN *has gone to* PROCTOR.)

WALLACE. And him? (*Looking at* MATHEW.)

DRAKE. If he can wield a sword.

LOGAN. He's wielded knives with skill before.

WALLACE. Then, welcome ... comrades ...

DRAKE. We'll make for Cleet.

WALLACE. Tell them of our plans.

O'HALLORAN. And the remuneration, we hear, is very grand.

DRAKE. A better world!

LOGAN. A better world.

O'HALLORAN. A better world.

LOGAN. It's come to that.

(*They move off.*
Light fades.)

Scene 5

Light comes up.
    CLEET *sits alone.*
    WALLACE *comes in.*

WALLACE. They're here.

(CLEET *gestures to send them in.* BROOME *enters, followed by* KENNEDY.)

BROOME. We've come with terms.

CLEET. I need no terms.

KENNEDY. We hold the towns; we hold all the major routes and forts.

CLEET. And little else ... you have no food. You've burnt up all the fields ...

BROOME. Nevertheless we come with terms ... The state offers you a coalition.

CLEET. I need no coalition ... coalesce with what? The people are disaffected ... Look through these woods ... an army made up from all your towns and forts ... The battle's lost. Take off your medals. Join with us. Generals and captains are not political men. We hold no grudge. Exchange your uniform for one of ours and we'll march together to the city wall and proclaim our confederacy with such a shout that tyranny itself will come running out. What say you, men?

BROOME (*looks to* KENNEDY. *Then:*) Aye ...

CLEET. And you?

KENNEDY. Aye ... Where the people lead ... Then order follows.

    (*Light fades.*)

Scene 6

Light comes up.
  PROCTOR *sits on a stone, alone.*
  JOAN *comes in.*

JOAN. The fool is ill.
    (PROCTOR *doesn't stir.*)
  I can't make out the cause.

PROCTOR. His mind has used him well ... Depriving him of speech and thought.
    (JOAN *leads* MATHEW *on in a drooping condition.*)

JOAN. I think he sickens for what he had before.

PROCTOR. He sickens for his illness, then.

JOAN. I'll take him back ... We'll join the others ... Build up, if not the old place, something new.

PROCTOR. Bend with the wind ... While I sit like a rock ... take on each storm as if it were the last ...

JOAN. But come with us ...

PROCTOR. Like donkeys to a mill ... Round ... and round ... and round, and round.

JOAN. See: the idiot has brought us back his smile.

PROCTOR. Aye ... he recognizes his fellow madmen well.

JOAN. The fruits of the labour, not the labouring, you thought were our reward.

PROCTOR. Does a man not set his eyes on the things he's laboured for?

JOAN. No more than on a child that he sends out from his door: not his, but her life is the thing he's struggled for.

PROCTOR. It denies the principal thing in men ...

JOAN. It denies their arrogance and pride.

PROCTOR. Aye ... but see new masters take up the things they won ... new towns, new farms, new forts ... new troops—old troopers with fresh harness on.

JOAN. Let leaders lead: direct us as they will—support the good, and fight against the ill ... what can't be taken is our joy in work ... our life, like theirs, is forfeit in the end.

(PROCTOR *shakes his head*.)

But what you looked for was a kind of death—the uniform at first, and then a home—inviolable extremes that like a hearse can take you safely to a given end.

PROCTOR. I'll have no more of living as it comes ... I must have goals, and ways and means ... if men are victims what value are the things they struggle to?

JOAN. I'll leave you here.

PROCTOR. The fool has turned his back.

JOAN. He fights ... and works ... he sees his path ...

PROCTOR. But inches from his head ... I look for further goals than that.

JOAN. The goal is in his heart ... and mine.

PROCTOR. Aye ... Well mine is turned to some vaster place than that.

(*She turns.*
MATHEW *has already turned: she follows him.*
Light fades.)

Scene 7

Light comes up.
  PROCTOR *is kneeling.*
  O'HALLORAN *and* LOGAN *enter.*

O'HALLORAN. A preacher ...

LOGAN. Or a hermit.

O'HALLORAN. The place is wild at that.

LOGAN. The search for work has taken us further than we
    thought.

O'HALLORAN. Away, or nearer ...

LOGAN. The searching's all that counts.

O'HALLORAN. Your honour, then ...
    (PROCTOR *stirs.*)

LOGAN. What prays your honour to, so well?

PROCTOR. I pray to God.

O'HALLORAN. The one above ...

LOGAN. Or the one we see around?

PROCTOR. I pray to be illuminated, friend.

O'HALLORAN. Illuminated? ... If the place isn't dark enough.
    He's right.

PROCTOR. This place is always dark.

LOGAN. Couldn't you find a lighter place, your grace, than
    this?

PROCTOR. No place is lighter than the one I'm in.

O'HALLORAN. To God ...

LOGAN. Another disaster.

O'HALLORAN. Struck again!
  (PROCTOR *prays*.)
LOGAN. Your honour ...
O'HALLORAN. Has illumination been forthcoming, then?
PROCTOR. In part.
  (*Prays*.)
LOGAN. He prays again.
PROCTOR. I look for illumination ...
O'HALLORAN. Yes?
PROCTOR. Of goals ... of where we go ... Of ends.
LOGAN (*to* O'HALLORAN). One end, illuminated, I should
  think, is not unlike the next.
  (*They laugh between themselves.* PROCTOR *prays*.)
O'HALLORAN. And when the end's illuminated, sir, what
  then?
PROCTOR. When the goal is clear the path is straight.
LOGAN. To God ... but he's wrapped up in his thoughts
  again.
O'HALLORAN. Ah ... see.
LOGAN. No, no ...
O'HALLORAN. He's raised his head.
LOGAN. Is that the way ...
O'HALLORAN. No ... no.
LOGAN. It's raised again ...
O'HALLORAN. No ...
LOGAN. No ...
  (*He gazes off*.)
PROCTOR. If you wish to know the path ... then follow me.
O'HALLORAN (*gazing off*). No end in view, as far as I can see.
  (PROCTOR *has risen and is moving off*.)
LOGAN. We might ...
O'HALLORAN. Follow?
LOGAN. At a distance, then.
  (PROCTOR *has gone off*.)

75

O'HALLORAN. To God ...
  (LOGAN *gazes off*.)
  I heard a lion roar.
LOGAN. Not that ...
O'HALLORAN. But look.
LOGAN. 'Tis the wildness of the man himself.
O'HALLORAN. A sword ...
LOGAN. 'Tis fashioned from a plough.
O'HALLORAN. A gun.
LOGAN. He waves them by his head.
O'HALLORAN. A crowd ...
LOGAN. His path is straight.
O'HALLORAN. Just see the troopers drop their swords and
  run.
LOGAN. A revolution.
O'HALLORAN. The wrath of God.
LOGAN. To Jesus! ...
O'HALLORAN. The massacre's begun.
  (*Pause*).
LOGAN. I see no one but the man himself.
O'HALLORAN. And all those things like stones ...
LOGAN. Heads.
O'HALLORAN. And all those things that waved ...
LOGAN. Hands.
O'HALLORAN. God ...
LOGAN. The majesty ...
O'HALLORAN. One voice.
  (*A dishevelled Crowd come on.*)
LOGAN. Do you travel from the place, or run?
FIRST TRAVELLER. We were driven out.
SECOND TRAVELLER. We had no choice.
FIRST TRAVELLER. The land was ruled by men before.
SECOND TRAVELLER. The one who rules it now is God.
FIRST TRAVELLER. All were equal in the land before.

SECOND TRAVELLER. Now those who deal in justice suffer by the sword.

THIRD TRAVELLER. Preference now is bestowed on those who seek it most.

FIRST TRAVELLER. He lives by intuition.

SECOND TRAVELLER. A magic voice.

THIRD TRAVELLER. And stands enhaloed by the sun.

FIRST TRAVELLER. No presence but his own commands.

O'HALLORAN. But here come rebels ...

CROWD. Aye.

THIRD TRAVELLER. The levellers rise again ... they flood the land and grow, in wood and grove ... inspired by injustice and longings for revenge.

(*The Crowd and Travellers go.*)

O'HALLORAN. The light grows dim ...

LOGAN. The woods ...

O'HALLORAN. The very trees ...

LOGAN. The streams ...

O'HALLORAN. The grassy mounds.

LOGAN. Have risen ...

O'HALLORAN. And fallen on the king ...

LOGAN. He flees ...

O'HALLORAN. And we flee ...

LOGAN. To a lighter place than this.

(*They go.*
Dark.)

Scene 8

Light comes up.
   PROCTOR *stands alone.*
   Some distance off, the BOATMAN.

77

JOAN *enters with* MATHEW.

JOAN. I see you've found the place.

PROCTOR. I have.

JOAN. Where the powerless and the unworldly meet.

PROCTOR. I dreamed I took conviction down to hell ... cleansed and bathed its empty shell ... and when I drank I found its contents turned to blood.

JOAN. Boatman ... shall we cross the stream?

(*They embark: move, stay still. The* BOATMAN *poles.*)

PROCTOR. Boatman: do we cross the stream?

BOATMAN. Aye.

PROCTOR. The land behind is dark.

JOAN. The one in front is darker still.

PROCTOR. Boatman, do you know these shores?

BOATMAN. The stream is all I know ... its shoals, its rocks, its crevices ... its gleams ... the pattern of its light at dawn and dusk ... the rushing of its waves ... its stillness when it floods or lies, dwindling, in a summer heat ... I know the river, and the manner of the boat; that's all.

(LOGAN *and* O'HALLORAN *have entered.*)

PROCTOR. Two figures stand upon that side.

BOATMAN. Aye ... two travellers whom I've seen before.

O'HALLORAN (*calling*). To God ... but boatman ...

LOGAN (*calling*). Boatman ... take us too.

PROCTOR. Can't you hear them? ... Guide it back.

BOATMAN. The price they never have ... nor mean to pay ... They hang like leeches to the things that others have ... hands which always receive can offer nought.

PROCTOR. Would you take our advancement to haul the men across?

BOATMAN. Each must find his own, my friend ... See: the two are already drifting back: the shore holds out distractions too ...

78

PROCTOR. Do you know the other shore?

BOATMAN. Some say it lightens beyond its darkest fringe ... others that it presages but a thicker darkness still.

JOAN. And the ones who travel back?

BOATMAN. No one who crosses ever comes this way again.
(*They disembark.*)

JOAN. See ... the boat has drifted in the stream ...

PROCTOR. He plies the oar ...

JOAN. For the first time in our lives we have no turning back.

PROCTOR. Fool: to the front ...

JOAN. He plunges in the dark.

PROCTOR. The darkness thickens ...

JOAN. Do you hear those cries and shouts?

PROCTOR. Are others moving in those fields that we knew before?

JOAN. And beyond the darkness ...

PROCTOR. Do you see the light?
(*Fade.*)